A Kid's Guide to
INCREDIBLE TECHNOLOGY™

The Incredible Story of Skyscrapers

Greg Roza

The Rosen Publishing Group's
PowerKids Press™
New York

For Autumn

Published in 2004 by The Rosen Publishing Group, Inc.
29 East 21st Street, New York, NY 10010

First Edition
Editor: Kathy Kuhtz Campbell
Book Design: Mike Donnellan

Illustration Credits: Leonello Calvetti, Alessandro Bartolozzi, Lorenzo Cecchi, Donato Spedaliere.
Photo Credits: p. 4 (left) © Underwood & Underwood/CORBIS; pp. 4 (right), 7 © Bettmann/CORBIS; p. 8 by Cindy Reiman; pp. 12, 20 © Michael S. Yamashita/CORBIS; p. 15 (left) © Robin Moyer/TimePix; p. 15 (right) © Paul Thompson/CORBIS; p. 16 © Thornton-Tomasetti Engineers; p. 19 © Yann Arthus-Betrand/CORBIS.

Roza, Greg.
The incredible story of skyscrapers / Greg Roza.— 1st ed.
    v. cm.— (A kid's guide to incredible technology)
Includes index.
Contents: The origin of the skyscraper—What makes a building a skyscraper?—On solid ground—Skyscraper skeleton—Skyscraper skin—Putting it together—The Empire State Building—The Citicorp Center—The Petronas Towers.
  ISBN 0-8239-6716-6 (library binding)
1. Skyscrapers—Juvenile literature. [1. Skyscrapers.] I. Title. II. Series.
  TH1615 .R69 2004
  720'.483—dc21

                                                                            2002153457

Manufactured in the United States of America

Contents

The Birth of the Skyscraper

Before the 1880s, most buildings in the United States were made mainly of stone or brick. Stone walls had to be very thick to hold up the weight of a building, so most office buildings were no taller than about seven **stories**, or about 84 feet (25.6 m) high.

In 1871, a fire destroyed much of Chicago, Illinois. When the city was rebuilt, **architects** used new **technology** to make the city's buildings taller and stronger. Steel frames carried the buildings' weight, which meant walls could be thinner, with more windows. After Elisha Otis showed that an elevator was safe to carry people in 1854, architects included elevators in their buildings. By the mid-1890s, some U.S. cities had buildings that were 22 stories tall, or about 302 feet (92 m) high. The buildings seemed to scrape the sky. People were soon calling them skyscrapers.

Left: *Many people consider the Home Insurance Building in Chicago to be the first true skyscraper. Finished in 1885, it was the first building to have both a steel frame and an elevator.* Right: *The 1871 Chicago fire destroyed about 18,000 buildings.*

Drawing Plans and Construction

Many steps must be completed before a skyscraper can be built. The owner who will have the skyscraper built needs to hire an architect to **design**, or plan, the building. This architect must take into account several details before he or she can make drawings or **blueprints** of the finished building. Some of these details include knowing about the land where the building will stand and understanding how the building will be used. For example, will the skyscraper be a place where people live, work, or shop, or a mix of these? After the architect has studied all parts of the project and has made the blueprints, the owner hires a construction company. This company includes many laborers, such as steel workers, plumbers, electricians, and other special workers. The construction company builds the building, based on the blueprints and the **materials**.

Left: An architect's plan shows from above how one floor of one of the Petronas Twin Towers in Malaysia should look. Right: Starting on March 17, 1930, workers built the 102-story Empire State Building at a rate of 4 ½ stories each week.

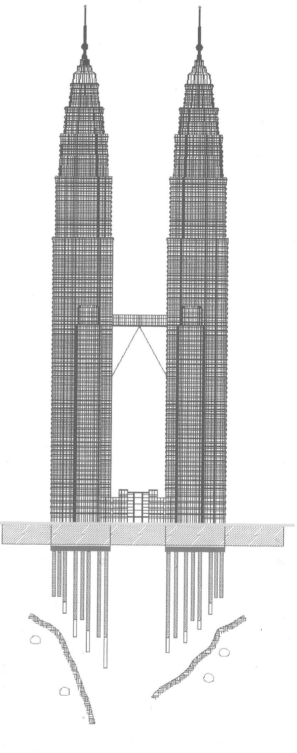

On Solid Ground

Building a strong, solid **foundation** is the first step in building a skyscraper. Without a strong foundation, the skyscraper could sink into the ground or could even fall over. To build a foundation, builders dig a large hole into the soil until they reach a hard layer of rock called **bedrock**. They use special construction methods to add **concrete columns** or steel **piers** that will give extra support to tall buildings. For some large skyscrapers, they make a watertight enclosure, or "bathtub," for the basements so that they will not fill with water. The foundation walls are built inside this bathtub. Most foundation walls are made of concrete. The space within some skyscrapers' foundations and basements can include underground parking garages, shopping areas, and even subway stations and tracks.

Left: *This New York City building's foundation has walls of concrete with steel bars for extra support.* Right: *This illustration shows the Petronas Twin Towers' foundations and the piers that were added to give the buildings a sturdy base.*

Skyscraper Skeleton

A skyscraper's frame, or skeleton, is made of **horizontal** steel beams and **vertical** columns. These beams and columns are joined together to form a cagelike frame that provides support for the skyscraper. A steel or **reinforced concrete** backbone, called the core, runs vertically through the middle of most skyscrapers to make the building stronger. The foundation supports the frame, which rises many stories above the ground. The skeleton must be very strong and stiff to support the weight of the building materials and the weight of people and furniture. Early skyscrapers were built with steel columns throughout the skeleton. These columns took up a lot of room. In the 1960s, architects invented tube frames. In tube frames, nearly all the steel columns are on the building's outer edges. Chicago's 1,127-foot- (343.5-m-) high John Hancock Center uses tube frames in its skeleton.

Just as a backbone supports a body, a core gives strength to a skyscraper and helps it to bear its weight. This cutaway view shows one of the Petronas Twin Towers. The tower's core includes concrete walls, stairs, and spaces for elevators, pipes, heating and cooling systems, and electric and telephone wiring.

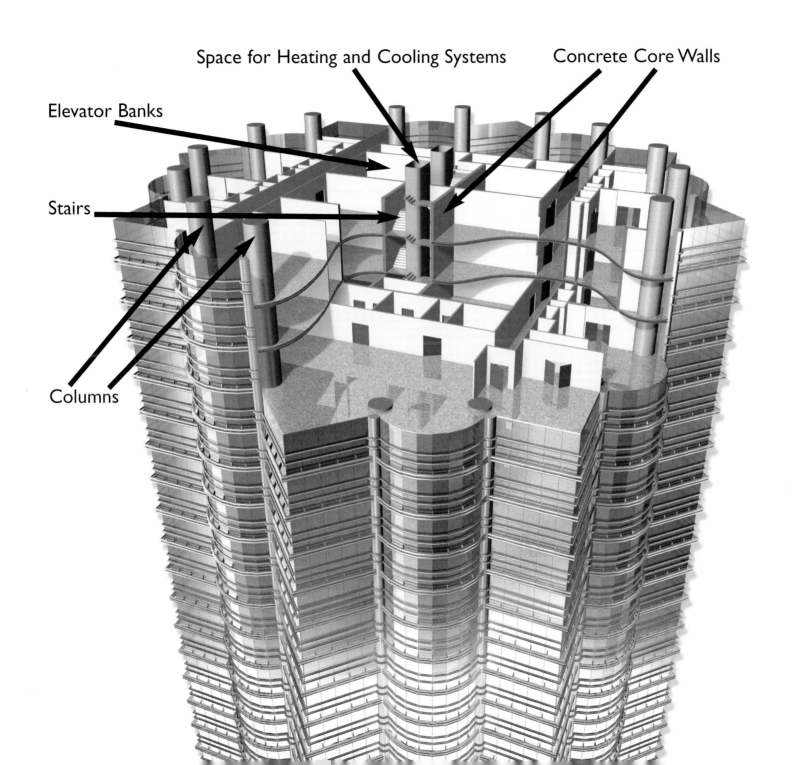

Space for Heating and Cooling Systems

Concrete Core Walls

Elevator Banks

Stairs

Columns

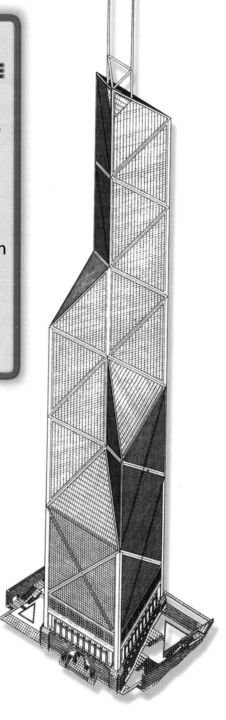

The Curtain Wall

A skyscraper's steel frame must be covered with outer walls. The outer walls are usually made of stone, glass, or a metal called aluminum. They hold up only their own weight and do not support the rest of the building's weight, which is the steel frame's job. A skyscraper's outer wall is often called the curtain wall, or the skin. This is because its chief purpose is to cover the building, allow for windows, and protect the building's contents from the weather. To make construction quicker, some parts of the curtain wall are made at another location. When they are needed, these parts are brought to the skyscraper and are snapped into place, like toy building blocks. Many modern skyscrapers, such as the Bank of China Tower in Hong Kong, China, have walls made of glass panes that are held in place by aluminum frames.

Left: The glass curtain walls of the Trump Tower in New York City let a large amount of natural light into the skyscraper. Right: The glass walls of Hong Kong's Bank of China Tower have steel bars called trusses that join to form a series of triangles and diamonds. The trusses help the building to withstand high winds.

Putting It Together

A skyscraper's columns and beams are raised into place with cranes. Then they are bolted and **welded** together. Cranes called tower or climbing cranes and moving cranes called mobile cranes help to raise steel beams, concrete, and other building materials to workers on the floor that is being built. A mobile crane helps to build the tower crane by lifting the tower crane's working arm into position so that crews can put the tower crane together. As the skyscraper gets taller, workers add sections to the tower crane as needed. As some workers build the upper floors, others work to finish the lower floors. Workers use cranes to lower metal floors into the frame. The floors are covered with concrete. Carpenters put up walls to make rooms. After the frame and walls are done, specially trained workers add plumbing, electrical and telephone systems, heating and cooling systems, and elevators.

Top: Tower cranes are seen here at the top of the Petronas Twin Towers during their construction in the late 1990s. Bottom: Tower cranes are used by construction workers to lift steel beams, concrete columns, building materials, and tools. A crane cannot be more than 265 feet (80.8 m) tall without some kind of support or it will tip over.

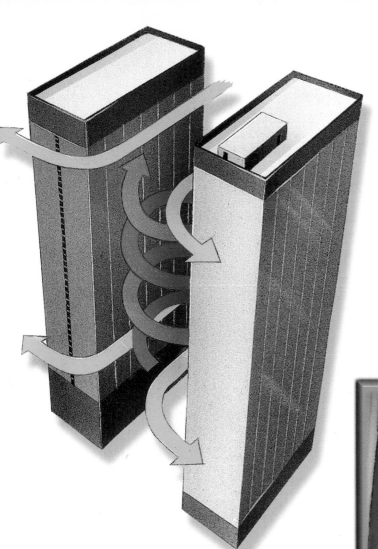

TECH KNOWLEDGE

New York City's Citicorp Center, completed in 1977, was the first skyscraper built with a TMD. The TMD at the top of the Citicorp Center weighs 400 tons (362.9 t).

Skyscrapers and Forces of Nature

The force of wind pushing against a building can make it sway, causing **tension** in the building's frame. Too much tension can pull the frame apart. To oppose the tension, many skyscrapers are equipped with a device called a Tuned Mass Damper (TMD). A TMD is a heavy concrete block made for one of the skyscraper's top floors. When the building sways one way, the block sways in the opposite direction. The swaying block dampens, or reduces, the building's movement, which can be caused by high winds or an earthquake. An earthquake is a force of nature that can create enough ground movement to tear a building's frame apart. In areas where earthquakes occur, skyscrapers are made to move with the quake. However, they must be strong so that they hold their shape and do not fall apart.

Top: *Wind blowing against and between skyscrapers creates powerful forces. Some skyscrapers sway in the wind so much that people on the upper floors can get motion sickness.* Bottom: *This is the TMD at the top of the 50-story Chifley Tower in Sydney, Australia. The TMD is located where the building's sway is the greatest.*

17

The Empire State Building

Perhaps the most famous skyscraper of all time is the Empire State Building in New York City. The Empire State Building is 1,224 feet (373.1 m) tall and has 102 stories. Its steel frame alone weighs about 60,000 tons (54,431.1 t). That is about three times as much steel as the 20,961 tons (19,015.5 t) that were used to build New York City's Chrysler Building. The 77-story Chrysler Building had been the tallest building in the world before the Empire State Building was completed in 1931. The Empire State Building held this title for 41 years.

All together the Empire State Building weighs about 365,000 tons (331,122.4 t). All that weight pushes down on the foundation, which causes a force called **compression**. The Empire State Building would fall apart if its frame and foundation were not strong enough to withstand that much compression.

Left: *The skin of the Empire State Building is made of steel, Indiana limestone, granite, and aluminum. There are about 10 million bricks in the Empire State Building.*
Right: *This illustration shows the Empire State Building and part of its blueprint.*

TIMELINE

1854 Elisha Otis shows the passenger-safe elevator in New York.

1870 The Equitable Building in New York City becomes the first office building to feature an elevator.

1871 A fire destroys many buildings in Chicago, Illinois. This event leads to the development of the first skyscrapers as Chicago is rebuilt.

1885 The Home Insurance Building in Chicago, Illinois, is the first building to have both an elevator and a steel frame, making it the first skyscraper.

1931 The Empire State Building is completed in New York City after one year and forty-five days of building.

1977 The Citicorp Center is completed in New York City. It is the first skyscraper to feature a Tuned Mass Damper (TMD).

1998 The Petronas Twin Towers are completed in Kuala Lumpur, Malaysia.

2004 The Taipei Financial Center in Taipei, Taiwan, is finished.

The Petronas Twin Towers

In 1998, the Petronas Twin Towers in Kuala Lumpur, Malaysia, became the tallest buildings in the world. Made of concrete and steel, each tower has 88 stories. About 558 feet (170.1 m) above the street, a double-decker skybridge connects the Petronas Twin Towers. This skybridge, which joins the two towers at the forty-first and forty-second floors, makes it easier to travel between the towers. When the wind is strong, the towers sway. To keep the bridge from being torn apart by the swaying towers, it is supported by two legs that are connected to the towers with movable ball joints. The 827-ton (750.2-t) skybridge is held up by two sets of legs. The legs are joined to the towers at the twenty-ninth floors. When the towers sway, the legs' slopes change and the bridge rises or sinks. The bridge itself has panels that get bigger. The bridge can sway as the towers sway.

Left: *The shape of the 1,483-foot-tall (452-m-tall) Petronas Twin Towers is based on an eight-pointed star, which has been an important symbol to Malaysians throughout their history.* Right: *The skin of the Petronas Twin Towers is made of 828,821 square feet (77,000 sq m) of glass and 699,654 square feet (65,000 sq m) of stainless steel.*

What Is Next for Skyscrapers?

How tall can architects build skyscrapers? Many architects and builders believe that they have the technology to build skyscrapers taller than the Petronas Twin Towers. For example, builders in Taipei, Taiwan, will finish the Taipei Financial Center, also called Taipei 101, in 2004. Taipei 101 will have 101 stories and will be 1,667 feet (508.1 m) tall. The skyscraper will have the fastest elevators on Earth, taking only 39 seconds to reach the eighty-ninth floor. Builders in Hong Kong, China, plan to construct a 1,575-foot-high (480-m-high) skyscraper called Union Square by 2007. Union Square will be 108 stories high. Taipei 101 and Union Square will be the two tallest buildings in the world, but for how long?

Glossary

architects (AR-kih-tekts) People who create ideas and plans for buildings.

bedrock (BED-rok) The solid rock found below the soil.

blueprints (BLOO-prints) The plans or drawings that show how a building will be made.

columns (KAH-lumz) Tall, thin posts that are used to help hold up a building.

compression (kum-PREH-shun) A force that squeezes objects together.

concrete (KON-kreet) A mix of water, stones, sand, and a special gray powder. Concrete becomes very hard and strong when it dries.

design (dih-ZYN) The plan or the form of something.

foundation (fown-DAY-shun) The part of a building on which other parts are built.

horizontal (hor-ih-ZON-til) Level and flat. The floor of a building is horizontal.

materials (muh-TEER-ee-ulz) What something is made of.

piers (PEERZ) Pillars, beams, and posts used to hold up something in an up-and-down direction.

reinforced concrete (ree-in-FORSD KON-kreet) Concrete that has been strengthened with steel bars or mesh.

stories (STOR-eez) The floors of a building. Buildings are often measured by the numbers of stories they have.

technology (tek-NAH-luh-jee) The way that a people do something using tools, and the tools that they use.

tension (TEN-shun) A stretched condition.

vertical (VER-tih-kul) In an up-and-down direction.

welded (WELD-ed) Used heat to melt pieces of metal together.

Index

Web Sites

Due to the changing nature of Internet links, PowerKids Press has developed an online list of Web sites related to the subject of this book. This site is updated regularly. Please use this link to access the list:

www.powerkidslinks.com/kgit/skyscrap/